UN-CHRISTMAS CHA[ ]

UN-CHRISTMAS CHARACTERS

Verses by
Ralph Stephenson
Cartoons by Noel Watson

A Deirdre McDonald Book
Bellew Publishing
London

First published in 1993
by Deirdre McDonald Books
128 Lower Richmond Road
London SW15 1LN

Verses copyright © Ralph Stephenson 1993
Cartoons copyright © Noel Watson 1993

All rights reserved

ISBN 1 898094 02 0

Phototypeset by Wayzgoose
Printed and bound in Great Britain by Hartnolls Ltd

CONTENTS

Preface	vii
The Meteorologist	1
The Dog Lover	3
The Duettist	7
The Nurse	9
The Doctor	10
Cricketers	13
The Flautitht	15
The Cellist	17
The Yachtsman	21
The Bore	23
Girl with Green Eyes	24
The Addict	25
The Motorist	29
The Country Lover	30
The Elector	32
The Bookseller	35
The Commuter	36
The Secretary	39
The Careerist	40
The Poet	43
The Lawyer	45
Animal Rights Advocate	46
The Rambler	49
The Publisher	53

PREFACE

Why celebrate Christmas when there is so little of it? 'Christmas comes but once a year,' wrote the poet, Tomas Tusser. One day for Christmas leaves 364 days for matters Un-Christmas and gives us much more time for celebration.

That is where this album of verses comes in. Not one of its light-hearted characters has anything to do with Christmas.

Though perhaps they do have something 'Christmas' about them: a kind of innocent (or not so innocent) enjoyment, right for a season when even the most serious of us put on paper-hats and play on the floor with the children.

Therefore, if you are looking for a Christmas *or* an Un-Christmas present for friends or relatives — this will do in *both* cases. So — as Lewis Carroll's Humpty Dumpty said, referring to un-birthday presents — 'There's glory for you'.

THE METEOROLOGIST
Thoughts of a . . .

With the aidio
Of the radio
Or newer
On the viewer,
I give reports meteorological
Which *are* logical,
Though you may find you're sweltering
Instead of sheltering.
PLEASE DON'T get terser
If it's vice versa.

If you lack
A mac
Abstain
From going out in the rain,
But with an umbrella
Bella
Phooey
To *la pluie*.

A light drizzle
Is a swizzle —
Although it isn't stronger
It lasts longer.
Thunderstorms come down thickly
But they're over quickly.

The duck
's in luck
With feathers
For all weathers.

The summer sun
Is fun.
It brings a blush to peaches
On the beaches,
But for moral and medical reasons
Avoid over-exposure in all seasons.

If you're lost
When skis get crossed
Or holler
If snow gets down your collar,
Then ice is only fit
To cool your gin-and-it.
Otherwise leave ice and snow
To the Eskimo.

THE DOG LOVER

I'd love to have a canine friend,
A true companion who would lend
A patient ear to all my woes,
With lively eyes and nuzzling nose.
But then I think — and get dejected;
Could I live up to what's expected?

Could I provide the scented ease
Demanded by a Pekinese?
Or hold the intellectual floor
Against a Laureate Labrador?
Aristocratic, upper-class —
With many dogs you have to pass
A test of fitness and of tone —
The Afghan Hound won't share his bone
With *any* whipper-snapper human;
The Otter Hound likes rowing-blue men.
The Great Dane and the Samoyed
Deserve a Royal four-poster bed.
The Kerry Blue, you may assume,
Needs tasteful decor in each room.
The Corgi, Basset, Cairn and Chow
Would raise a most unholy row
If missing (nothing less or more)
Fine Persian carpets on the floor.
And as for food — good gracious me!
A Blenheim would be all at sea —
An Airedale would not understand —
If offered some INFERIOR BRAND.
And cooking — *cordon bleu* — or better
For Borzoi, Dachs or Irish Setter.
You could not think of serving SPAM
To Chihuahua or Sealyham!
Crockery also should be good
To match the quality of food:

Spaniel or Collie — ill 'twould bode
To serve in *anything* but Spode.
For collars, leashes and such gear
It's Bond Street — nowhere else I fear.
No noisy parties, not at night
Alsatians would not think it right —
So quiet and don't disturb the slumber
Of Bulldog, Terrier or Clumber.

But still — there is a brighter side
There are some dogs without such pride.
The pooch, the cur, the tyke, the pi
Will take low life as well as high.
They're mongrels just like YOU and ME;
They do not have a pedigree.
They do not have to watch their hips,
For supper they have steak and chips —
The difference they cannot tell
From *filet mignon maître d'hôtel.*
With them my courage would not fail,
They're said to read the *Daily Mail!*

So though TOP BREEDERS may prefer
An Afghan with expensive fur,
I'll settle for the common kind;
And I expect that then I'll find
They'll be as brave and bright and true
As any dog whose blood is blue
And bite the burglar down below
As hard as any aristo.

A patient ear to all my woes.

THE DUETTIST

It was a happy choice, no less
When I invited modest Bess
To play duets — Mozat and such —
She had such strong yet gentle touch,
That when our hands in music twined
Her image filled my heart and mind.

Primo, secondo, both we'd learn
Sharing the melody in turn,
And so with shy and beating hearts
We took both top and bottom parts,
Playing *legato* side by side
My heart to hers by phrasing tied.

At first, *adagio, andante,*
I told her that she took my fancy;
And then — *allegro* — with more haste
Put my arms — *presto* — round her waist.
Then kissed her and — pause, one bar rest —
My feelings — *dolce* — I confessed.

Then — double bar — what joy to tell,
She said: I feel for you as well.
Through Bach, Beethoven, Schumann, Brahms,
I learned her humours and her charms.
Playing Clementi, Ravel, Fauré,
Our love affaire went *con amore.*

I hope we may go on combined
With notes and hearts and arms entwined
Through sharps and flats, treble and bass,
Keeping — two-four, six-eight — one pace,
One time, one tempo and agree
With loving hearts one harmony.

Envoi
Unless th' piano-stool should break
And prove we'd made a big mistake.

THE NURSE

The nurse is a delightful but a frightening phenomenon;
She approaches you when you're in bed with nothing
but pyjamas on.

Whether you are old or young
She pushes an uncomfortable thermometer right underneath
your tongue.

To take your pulse she grasps your wrist between thumb
and finger.
You dare not malinger

Lest she report you to the doctor.
(She is a cross between an angelic vision and a
university proctor.)

Then with irreproachable vowels
Having tied you up in knots, she looks you straight in
the eye and asks embarrassing questions about your
bowels.

Her face and figure may look quite ravishing,
But her manner is cold and correct, her bust is starched,
And no compliments on you is she lavishing.

Florence Nightingale is the nurse's ideal
And Florence Nightingale (when she was bossing
them) to men did not appeal.

Therefore I conclude that the nurse is an adorable
but a terrifying apparition,
Because, though you feel she could be nice, you have
to do with her when you are in no condition.

THE DOCTOR

The DOCTOR has a stethoscope
And bottles full of dangerous dope.

Perhaps he has a high degree
(F R C S; M R C P)
Or p'r'aps he's only Ch. B.

With bedside manner sure to please
His little hammer taps our knees
In search of some obscure disease,
And now he rarely asks for fees.

Your symptoms in his files are noted.
His pills are often sugar-coated.
To his profession he's devoted.

Right from his very first dissection
The DOCTOR strives towards perfection
And for each ailment or infection
He has a tablet or injection.

Too busy giving patients doses
For hobbies such as growing roses,
His time is spent in diagnosis
Or clearing up our halitosis.

If puzzled by a situation
He'll recommend a consultation
Before commencing amputation.

Once as a Surgeon or Physician
He had a well-defined position,
But now research is so intense
The *kinds* of doctors are immense:

The Analyst has come to stay.
(For him you usually have to pay.)
He lists your thoughts from day to day
And charms your complexes away.

The Gynaecologist's ability
May help the sterile to fertility
Or playing quite another role
He may advise on birth-control.

Perhaps he'll practise just one -ectomy
These DOCTORS seem quite the elect to me.
Their skill in one sole operation
May be the wonder of the nation.

He may become an -ologist
Of which there is a longish list
(Malari-, Radi-, Bi-, Path-, Zoo-
Are five that will be known to you.)
And spend his life industriously
In studying his -ology.

Or he may work in Public Health
And do good as it were by stealth.
In this field there's a maxim sure:
Prevention better is than cure.

Or should he lean to the polemic
He may become an academic,
And use his special skill and knowledge
In teaching at a Students' College.

In tropical diseases too
The specialists have work to do,
And other lines are Diatetics,
Physiotherapy, Genetics,
Orthopaedics, work Forensic
Which has to do with Law and men sick.

But can the DOCTOR keep his head
Now he's tied up with tape that's red?
Or keep alive his healing skill
When snowed upon with forms to fill?

Patient fear not! He is no door-mat,
And any heavyweight bur-*eau*-crat
He'll have no serious trouble slighting,
For NOBODY can read HIS WRITING.

CRICKETERS

The amateurs of England
Pleb and aristocrat
Once put on pads and flannels
Then seized a cricket-bat,

Strode to the pitch,
Surveyed the field,
And (hearts right stout and true)
They struck the ball with mighty strokes
Into the azure blue.

The willow and the leather,
The googly, swerve and spin,
The off-drive and the on-drive,
And to be sure the batting side,
Were definitely IN.

But amateurs of Enland now
When cricketers go pro
Seize fiddle, drum and breezy flute
And scrape and strike and blow.

The soft recorder sounds in schools
And harpsichords no longer mute
Are played — though not by 'muddied oafs'
Or even 'flannelled fools'.

Alas! Today the flannelled chaps
(The pros you can't except)
Are busy missing catches
And proving less adept.

The BBC may lend support
Broadcasting ball-by-ball,
It's not reflected in the sport
The wickets simply fall.

Their great play comes in snatches,
And they're good — at LOST TEST-MATCHES.*

*Stop press (August '93): for 'lost' read 'last'.

THE FLAUTITHT
From a Lthping Lover

When dearetht ELTHPETH I do kith
It fillth me full with keenetht blith.
When theth away her quipth I mith.
The hath no vithe — all virtueth nithe.

Were I a Dover Thole, I'd with
With all my heart the were a fith,
A glittering and lovely fith,
Thwimming around — not on a dith.

I lithp her praitheth night and day,
Nothing too muth that I can thay.
I think of her ath kin and kith,
A willowy and thoulful mith,
Playing the flute with thkill and art
With airy lipth and thmiling heart.
Tho even if thome noteth theem wrong
I therenade her thtill in thong.

THE CELLIST

O Cello, drone and buzz like bees,
    Pure honey,
Sitting snug between my knees.

Soar to treble, plunge to bass
    Versatile,
Change in clef and pitch and pace.

You're a friend to understand,
    My pal,
Warmest member of the band.

Violins are far too proud,
    Oh, my deah!
Snobs who look down on the crowd.

Violas can be sour at heart,
    Grr! Grr!
Jealous for the leading part.

While cellos sit there quite possessed
    Sweet content,
To form a platform for the rest.

Flutes go piping, thin and cold
    Miaou!
Skinny little things to hold.

Who could be fond of clarinets?
    Those reeds,
Such temperamental martinets.

The bassoon is a hubbly-bubbly
    Blurb! Blurb!
Gurgling in a sonic subway.

The brasses are a vulgar lot,
        Poop-a-doop!
Trombones to trumpets playing 'hot'.

The double-bass may be reliant
        Full of steroids,
But who could fall for such a giant?

Whether big drum or glockenspiel
        Percussion,
Or great bells chiming, peal on peal —

They strike my eardrums and they go
        Bang! Bang!
Over my head in blow by blow.

They've all got points, but faults besides
        Poor things,
Except the cello which abides
        My pal.

So cello drone and buzz like bees
        Pure honey,
And stay there snug between my knees.

THE YACHTSMAN
Then and Now

A wet sheet and a flowing sea,
A wind that follows fast
And fills the white and rustling sail
And bends the gallant mast.

The sail got jammed. We couldn't get it up or down . . .

Hell, was I sick? The boat stood on her head . . .

Then Sal fell overboard. Dead drunk again . . .

That bastard Harry? Don't go out with him . . .

So you've been stuck in that mud too . . .

The blank insurance didn't cover it . . .

He isn't any good with engines . . .

Always scrounging drinks . . .

Damn boat? I'm selling it . . .

Gales in the Channel . . .

We missed the tide . . .

Sailing's lovely . . .

Sailing . . .

Sailing . . .

THE BORE

Alas! It is not any use
To snub the friendly fly.
Jests, taunts and even mild abuse
Will not drive him away.
He buzzes madly in your face,
You toss a restless head
And roughly, rudely change your place
And turn your back instead.
Peste! Monsieur Mouche thinks it is play
And tickles all your vertebrae.
You cannot argue with the fly
Or say you don't feel well,
Or that a rendez-vous is nigh,
Or simply — GO TO HELL.
Each insult makes him buzz with glee
He finds you rather cute.
He waits for no invite to tea,
He simply dips his snoot.
His social hide is inches thick
The boring, brash, unfeeling tick.
The only way with such a bore
To get the truth into his head —
It is to raise the fly-swat high
And swat — and swat him DEAD.

GIRL WITH GREEN EYES

Traffic lights show Stop and Go
Red and Green and Amber glow.
But the light of Paradise
Shines constant in my Mary's eyes.

THE ADDICT

His furrowed brow, his abstract looks
As he dips into reference books,

Proclaim the addict in full flight
Musing on each mis-leading light,

Intent on T-ing every square,
Tracking the *emu* to its lair.

He's tickled by each witty pun:
A swindled bailiff must be *dun*;

A bright child, some would say, is *sun*;
A single prize — there to be *one*.

At anagrams he may turn pale:
Evil, live, Levi, vile, or *veil.*

By hidden words he may be bitten:
Roast crackling's found in pu*p or k*itten.

His animals, four-footed clues:
Are *okapis* or (stop-press) *gnus*.

With palindromes is he in tune:
Eye, madam, sexes, boob or *noon*?

The French he finds are *le, la, les,*
A can of flour he hears is *May*.

Four-letter words are proper here
From flattering *fawn* to loving *deer*.

A master nut to turn is *head*.
We would join forces to be *we'd*.

The fiend behind these devious pranks,
Trickster whose wiles deserve few thanks,

Avoids a sure and sticky doom
By sheltering in a *nom-de-plume*;

Or even safer seeks to be
In total anonymity.

So beard the *setter* in his den,
Provide him with a fountain pen,

And force him by a bomb with fuse
To solve a puzzle WITHOUT CLUES.

THE MOTORIST
Advice to the Motorist

Confusion, pollution, congestion, delay —
Your costly new limmos have now had their day.

Fair-false-spoken wardens patrol through the town
With note-books to take your particulars down,
And hand out large fines for a minute's o'erstaying.
Grim wheel-clamps are ready to cause more delaying.

Garages now rook you near thirty an hour;
Insurance and road-tax are out of your power.
Knocks, scratches and bumps are quite often a *must*,
A few years of use and one day you'll see — rust!

Pedestrian precincts are steadily growing;
Great humps on the roadway stop fast traffic flowing;
Diversions abound and lane-closure is common;
(A parked car in Belfast — it might have a bomb on.)
Just joy-riding used to be innocent fun,
But now it's like running amok with a gun.

Long-distance — you go much too fraught for the view,
And then at the café wait hours in a queue.
Go fast and a flashing patrol-car will hail you
Then shortly a twenty-mile tail-back assail you.

Kerb-crawling and dates? Never mind what you're told.
Love's better in bed, and back-seats can be cold.

Imprisoned in seat-belts and dazzled by glare,
Ear-deafened by thunderous pop-on-the-air,
If then you're debating — or will you or won't?

ADVICE TO THE MOTORIST is, quite briefly, DON'T.

THE COUNTRY LOVER
Rush-hour Rhyme

When the weather I am und
I take no pleasure in Cent Lond
Nor, when depressed and full of care,
Laugh with the fountains in Traf Square.
I don't, when bowed with weight of work,
Cut capers in gay Piccy Circ,
Nor, when commuting gets too hard,
Enjoy the op at Covent Gard.
The Col, Sad Wells, too crowd I find
I'd rather spend my mon at Glynde.
The BR stats all make me sick —
Char Wat Eust Pad Liv Bake and Vic
And lux hotels seem like a lav
The Ritz, the Cumb, the Dorch, the Sav.
Department stores are simply gru —
Mark Spen, Wool, Self, Pete Jo, John Lew.
The bills may give a fatal shock
At Café Roy or Simps or Troc.
I do not even like the Mall
And give sour looks at square Buck Pal;
I would not take a taxi-cab
To see House Comm or Westmin Abb.
The crowded cit oppresses me
Even the dome of Wren's Saint P.

I long for wills, sycs, chests, and pops,
For vals and mounts, meads, thicks and cops,
For rabs and chicks and pups and kits,
For cucks and stars and robs and tits,
For an and veg, for flow and bud,
For bull with bell and cow with ud.
Time to relax and spend the night
In Guild or Camb or Cant or Bright.
For sport activ, for shoot fish hunt,
And leis to ramble in the countryside.

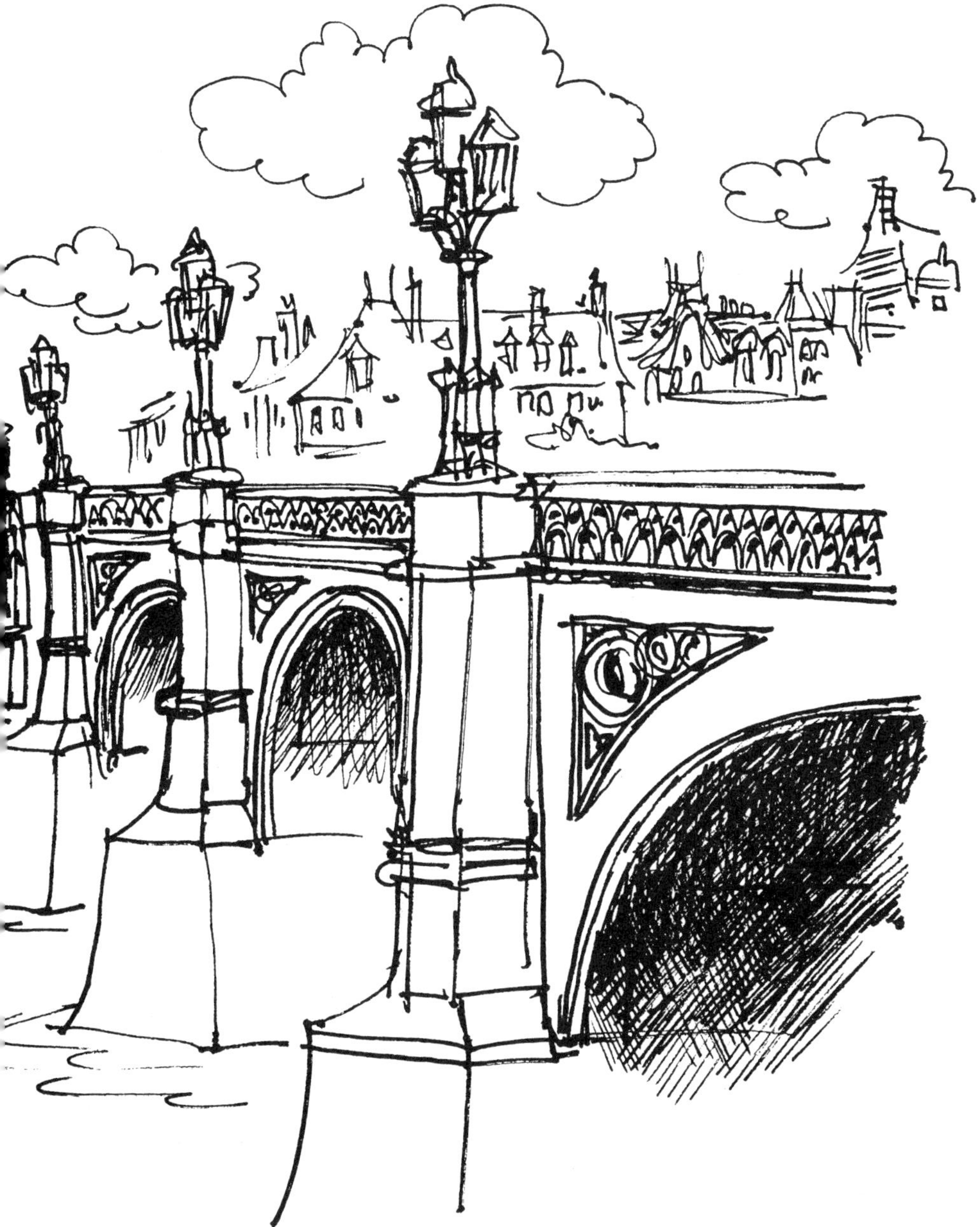

THE ELECTOR

Election Day!
I'm on my way,
I'll make my cross.
I will not toss,
But weigh each claim,
Ponder each name
And over tea
I'll try to see
The dame or gent
Who'll represent
The best in us
And make a fuss
About what's wrong
Taking a long,
Sagacious view
Of what's the true
Politic course.
Debate not force
Will one fine day
Show us the way
To Cornucopia
Utopia.

Not one of those
Who take the pose
Of 'What's the use
They've cooked our goose';
Who stay at home
To moan and groan
And lie awake
Seeing that lake
Of milk, that mount
Of butter; count
Inflation's rate;
Fear 'Somewhere-Gate',

While all the time
Increasing crime
Worries their mind.
If motoring kind
Find petrol's price
A crippling vice,
And British Rail
To no avail
'Cause fares are dear.
(What about beer!!)

BUT — p'r'haps they're RIGHT
To thus take flight?
Where e'er we go
Another blow.
WHY all around
Troubles abound!
Who then can cope?
How can we hope
That by a vote
We'll keep the boat
Safely afloat?
Or that a cross
Will stop its loss?

YES — too much wrong.
I feel less strong.
To rack my brain
May well be vain;
And so *I'll* stay
At home today —
Another ostrich or escaper
Reading more troubles in the paper.

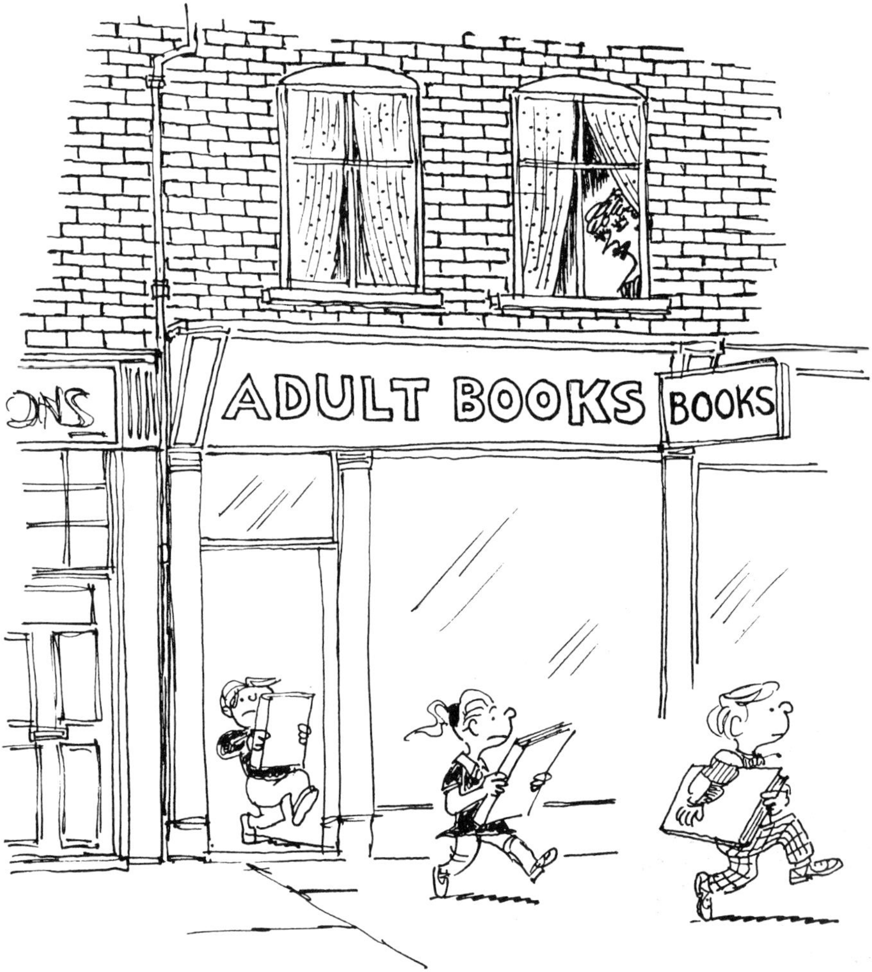
ADULT BOOKS
BOOKS

THE BOOKSELLER

CUSTOMER SPEAKS:

From Rising Sunny land I come
To England's raining, not-much sun.
That hard World Language I have learn
For those great author my soul yearn.
To make good friendship, my heart quicken,
With Shakespeare play and novel Dicken.
I am a very keen one for
Hardy and Keats and wits of Shaw.
Therefore in London I make bow
To City's heart — that is Soho,
And shop-book there I many spy
My fierce excitement going high.
Young lady stand with fetching looks
And see! Clearly those big sign — BOOKS.
But inside, damp my spirit fall
Not any Pope or Swift at all.
Picture of ladies — no-close-on
And all the author are ANON.

THE COMMUTER

Masks in the carriage — casual, grave or smiling
With talk, thought, book or paper, trip beguiling.
Behind, beneath each mask a world existing
Of rain and storm and wind and calm consisting.
Hearts beating, sad and happy, charged with feeling —
Desires, hopes, longing — future acts concealing,
Or else with past delights and disappointments living,
Ambitious, loving, hating, taking, giving.
On others' praise or blame or coldness dwelling;
Inventions, plans, ideas within them welling.
The air is thick with unseen passions beating
Despite each person's prim or casual seating.

How different is the world outside the train,
Free of emotion — fear or fret or pain.
    Serried houses bright as day
    From the carriage passing by,
    Roofs brushed in and chimneys spruce,
    Painters' pigments, rich and fresh.
    There a mother with a pram,
    There a mower on a lawn,
    There a Scottie bouncing gaily,
    There some greyhounds on their daily
    Walking exercise demure —
    All is colourful and pure.
    There are grasslands, flowers and trees
    Free from pests as gardener's dreams,
    Free from toil or disappointment
    Just vicarious enjoyment.
    Goats and horses, sheep and cows
    Painted gay as childhood toys.
    World with neither right nor wrong —
    Hill and sky and road far-flung.
    Motor-cars that move by magic
    Naught laborious or tragic.

Puppet people decorated
Clouds in shapes elaborated.
A picture universe is ours
Watching from our ivory towers.
How different is the world seen from the train,
Free from emotion — fear or fret or pain.

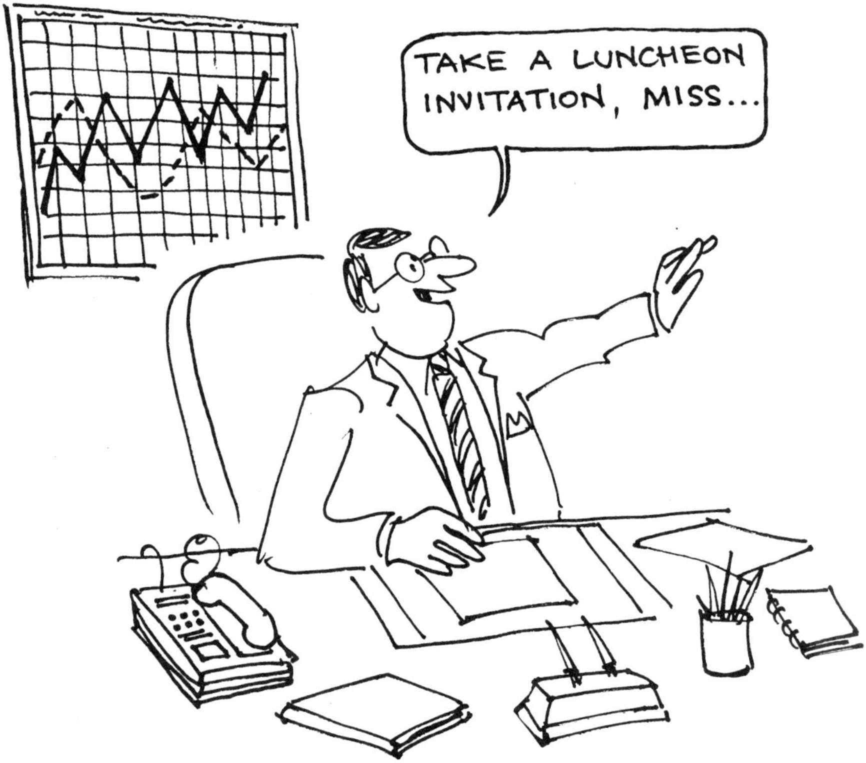
TAKE A LUNCHEON INVITATION, MISS...

THE SECRETARY — A BALLADE

She has every single hair in place, her salary is not high;
Her clothes are quite impeccable, her manner bound to please.
She takes dictation in a flash, she never asks you 'Why?'
She's punctual to the minute, she will charge no extra fees.
Her tastes are not extravagant, she lives on buns and teas;
Her eyes are wide and innocent, her face is quite unlined.
There's nothing more industrious, not even ants or bees;
She's a most efficient secretary with everything in mind.

If you ask her out to luncheon she will not tell a lie;
She may say 'yes' immediately and put you at your ease;
Or say with satisfaction that she's got another guy.
Perhaps she'll take offence and then the atmosphere will freeze;
Or she'll let you know tomorrow whether her mama agrees.
But whatever her reply is and however well she's dined,
She'll command the situation from the melon to the cheese.
She's a most efficient secretary with everything in mind.

Oh, is there any business man who can with truth deny
The time he's spent admiring silken secretaries' knees,
The time he's wasted chattering while golden moments fly
With girls who keep their perfect poise however he may tease?
They say that hardy mariners who sail the seven seas
Have girls in every port to which their ship its way may find,
But I'd rather be a business man, my reasons being these:
She's a most efficient secretary with everything in mind.

'Prince' she can spell and 'Princess' too, easy as shelling peas,
And will undertake commissions of the most exacting kind.
But at half-past-five or six o'clock she dons her coat and flees.
She's a most efficient secretary with everything in mind.

THE CAREERIST

Romantic Royals dwell in gorgeous palaces
While simple nomads sleep in humble tents.
House Agents live we really don't know whereabouts
Just call each Friday to collect the rents.

These are the enterprising ones I write about.
These are the models that we ought to watch.
Instead of potted shrimps and cheese and groceries
THEY deal in luxury flats and housing blocks.

They dress in smartly-tailored City reach-me-downs.
Their offices are spanking neat and clean.
Their pin-up photos proudly in the window dressed
Focus a freshly-blushing bridal dream.

Their boards (entirely free) our city decorate.
Their properties FOR SALE are all desirable.
They'll recommend a SURVEY independently —
Their honesty in this is quite admirable.

The rates they charge are not such high percentages
But then they're levied on quite large amounts,
So as their overheads tend to be moderate
They ought to show quite favourable accounts.

When younger I was going to be an astronaut,
An engine-driver or a circus clown,
A cricketer, a sprinter or an acrobat,
Even an academic in a gown.

But now I think for me the right profession
Is one I'll learn on reaching man's ESTATE,
Starting with cardboard boxes Metropolitan
And rising to the Mansions of the Great.

TERRACED or SEMI-DEE I'll have commodities
All creatures need — at least until they're dead —
Even the snail and tortoise with their carapace,
Even the oyster tucked into its bed.

Nor RISING DAMP, nor DRY ROT, will deter me;
KEYS to the Doorway of Success I'll hold.
Gaining with graft and grit VACANT POSSESSION,
HOUSE AGENCY will then be mine — I'm SOLD!!

GALE WARNING! GENTLY-KISSING WHISPERING BREEZES ARE EXPECTED IN ALL AREAS TONIGHT
WEATHER
TV

THE POET

Love's Tender Passion poets ever nurse
In chiming, sweet and sentimental —
                    iambics, dactyls, spondees etc.

First praise the skies that bring fresh Easter showers
To Spring's gay-coloured, heavy-scented —
                    sexual parts of plants.

Give thought to wanderers who oft-time dream
Of shady pool and babbling brook and —
                    flood damage a million.

Adore the gently-kissing, whispering breeze
That murmurs softly thru' the forest —
                    hurricane fury devastates woodland.

Long may this sea-girt land its Empire keep
O'er Neptunes mighty realm, the watery —
                    another tanker disaster.

Last — God's dear little ones, angels till seven,
Sent down all pure, a gift from highest —
                    sex education now compulsory in schools.

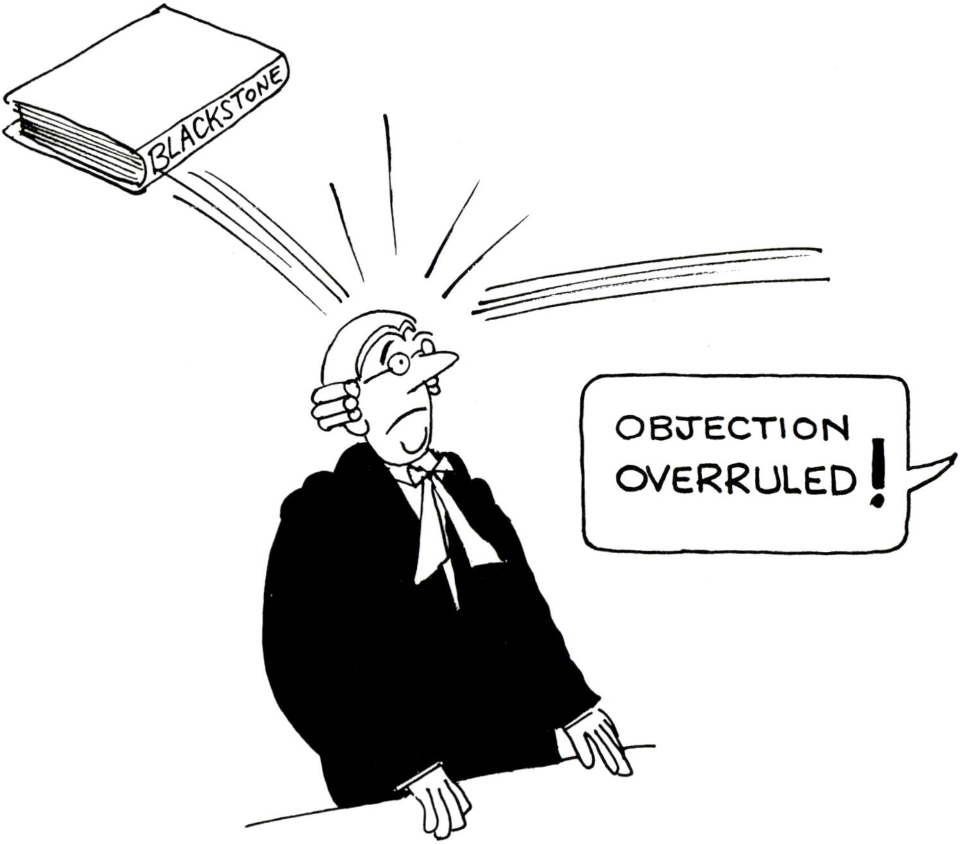
BLACKSTONE
OBJECTION OVERRULED!

THE LAWYER

The legal eagle is a bird
In courts and chambers often heard.
His voice is clear, his thought is sound,
His legal knowledge is profound.

Solicitors clarify your thoughts
And may appear in lower courts.
Conveyancing is their affair,
They'll check the title-deeds with care.
Arrange divorce or draft a will,
Or help you to collect a bill.

Barristers are another kind
Who have that keen debating mind.
They sport a wig, they wear a gown,
They'll grind a stubborn witness down.
To show their client should go free
They'll quote from Jones *v.* Smith '03.
They've Latin phrases at command
What you and me don't understand:
Like *actus reus* — what is done
Or *mens rea* — the way thoughts run.

But there are cynics — what a bore —
Who say you'd best avoid the law.
Bear minor set-backs with a smile
Rather than start a costly trial.
They'll even say — and lawyers vex —
Justitiam non curat lex.

ANIMAL RIGHTS ADVOCATE

Oh! Don't be rude to puppy dogs
Or say cross things to cats;
Show courtesy to jelly-fish
And be polite to sprats.

Put breadcrumbs out for pigeons;
Be kind my child, to birds
And do not meet a marmoset
With harsh or biting words.

Don't jump upon poor kangaroos;
Send best regards to hares
And even say a glad 'Good Day'
To large and grizzly bears.

Give helping hands to hammerheads.
Hold whales in high regard.
Pass by in peace all flocks of geese
And call all leopards 'Pard'.

Treat hens and roosters with respect.
Take off your hat to chicks
And do not not try to swat a fly
Or cockroaches or ticks.

Don't pull the legs of horses
Or disturb the sleep of bees;
In queues give way to rabbits
And do not powder fleas.

Be well behaved to living things;
Remember that my sweet.
Never be cruel to animals . . .
And eat up all your meat.

BEWARE
OF
THE BULL

THE RAMBLER
(Part One. Il Penseroso)

The Rambler homeward plods his weary Way
A Bull or Two have chased him on his Walk.
Missing the Foot-Path, very sad to say,
He and the Farmer had a little Talk.
He counted thirty Stiles — or rather more.
The Mud was Inches deep where Horses rode.
On barb-ed wire his Anorak he tore
(Too bad when he'd obeyed the Country Code).

The Path obstructed by a Field of Rape,
Half-a-Mile Detour added to his Toil,
From a fierce Dog contrived he to escape,
In a clay Field collected ploughed-up Soil.
With Beer two Pounds a Pint, his Lunch was dear,
Crisps were the only Food there was to eat.
While Chat and Music (Pop) assailed his Ear
The weary Rambler could not find a Seat.
Lunch over, he his ardent Way resumed,
But gentle Rain from Heaven joined his Stroll.
His Boots were water-proof, but he was doomed
And trod by Chance into a rain-filled Hole.
Horses and Cows looked on him in Amaze;
On Major roads indifferent Cars roared by;
From a lone Cottage came unfriendly Gaze
As if a Rogue or Vagabond were nigh.
'Neath lowering Skies, by tossing Trees he strove.
This was no fair Arcadian Scene,
There were no shapely Wood-Nymphs in the Grove.
Even forlorn of Golfers was the Green.

Then (as on outward Journey) comes the Strain
Of Engineering Works on British Rail:
A Train — a Bus — a Train — a Bus — a Train.
Sadly his buoyant Spirit 'gins to fail.
On reaching Home-Sweet-Home his Bath is cold,
An Oversight but still — he heaves a Sigh —
More Pleasures other Pastimes might well hold?
Then thinks? To Rambling give just one more Try?

THE RAMBLER
(Part Two. L'Allegro)

Hope-ful our Rambler ventures forth anew.
His Train on Time, full cheap his Day-Return.
Lush Meadows sparkling fresh with early Dew
Give him stout Heart and Energy to burn.
All Stiles are easy, pleasant is the Way,
A Lark sings tuneful in an azure Sky.
A *friendly* Farmer answers his 'Good Day',
His Step springs blithe, his morning Spirit high.
O'er Hill and Dale he goes, full light his Load,
Expectant Horses come to say 'Hello',
A cheerful Housewife smiles from her Abode,
And Dogs, tail-wagging, peaceful, see him go.
Past Cottage thatched to Tudor-timbered Inn
(British Tradition at its cosy Best)
Real Ale and Barmaids (bosomed) welcome him.
Our thirsty Traveller sits and drinks with Zest.
Lunch past, the rural Gods are friendly still,
A gentle Zephyr wafts from out the West,
Softly young Lambs bleat from a near-by Hill.
Arcadian Scene indeed. For there at rest
Sits shapely Wood-Nymph — lost, forlorn, alone,
Who asks, to find her Path, our Hero's Aid.
He — quite enchanted by her dulcet Tone —
Enthused agrees, and leads th' lovely Maid.
They talk, they laugh, their Interests are in Line,
Fair Kissing-Gates from Time to Time they meet.
Down Dangerous Slopes their Fingers intertwine,
She finds him brave, he finds her honey-sweet.

So now our Ramblers (plural) walk as One
No Doubt about the Sport they both prefer.
Within their Hearts an ever-smiling Sun.
She follows him? Not now. He follows her.

YOUR JUNGLE DESCRIPTIONS ARE VIVID, BUT YOUR DIALOGUE NEEDS POLISHING UP.........
MSS

THE PUBLISHER

PUBLISHER SPEAKS:

Bookmakers on the race-course need just horses, odds and chatter,
But making books for booksellers is quite another matter.

It is a complex business and requires quite many skills
And sometimes may involve a clash of interests or wills.

The *writers* are the start of it and authoring's their art;
Ideas are what they need or else emotions from the heart.

Then come the *literary agents* who do percentage deals,
They know *Important Publishers* and chat to them at meals.

Both may employ keen *readers* to tell their private thoughts
On manuscripts submitted and type out short reports.

As *publisher* I then decide if publishing's OK
For I'm the one with money and I have the final say.

Then *editors* (commissioning) can draft a contract deed
Setting out authors' royalties and other points at need.

Authors can't spell, can't punctuate and don't know grammar too,
So that is what the *copy editors* are there to do —

They look at structure, references, consistency and such,
They're walking know-alls and must have a very tactful touch.

Now come *designers, indexers,* and *artists* with their fees
(We seem to be collecting heaps and heaps of expertise).

But patience, for here come the most important ones to know:
(Their craft was started so they say five hundred years ago)

With *typesetters*, *lithographers*, good *printers* take a bow.
Today their technique's mechansied, computerised and how.

The proofs are read by *proof-readers* and whenthe *binding*'s over
The book's supplied by thousands, resplendent in its cover.

Reviewers write, *reps* take the stage to contact the last fellers
And they're the end of everything, the erudite *booksellers*.

SMALL VOICE SPEAKS:

Don't finish yet Great Publisher, may I suggest you need a —
A further (humble) character — and that's the *Common Reader*.

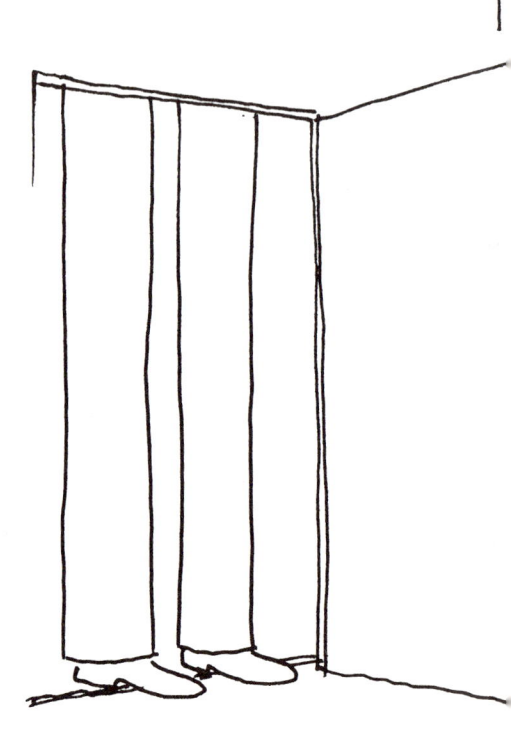

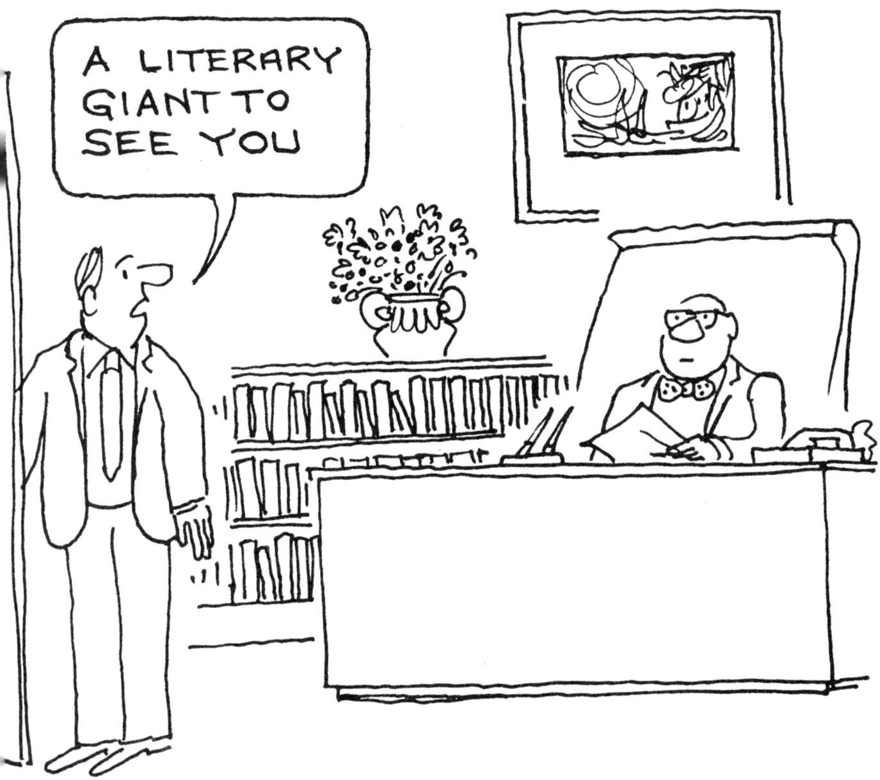
A LITERARY GIANT TO SEE YOU